MONEY $MART TEENS

MONEY $MART TEENS

TEENS

48 Interactive Lessons for Understanding, Making, Saving, and Spending Money

ALFRED D. RIDDICK, JR.

Game Time Budgeting, LLC
260 Northland Boulevard, Suite 300
Cincinnati, OH 45246
www.GameTimeBudgeting.com

Illustrated by IndieArtSpace
Interior design by Adina Cucicov
Edited by Shawanda Pauldin

ISBN: 978-0-9913929-2-6
Printed in the United States of America

To Bill Bagley, one of the most genuine people
I know. Thanks for taking a chance on me early in
my entrepreneurial career. I appreciate you!

Table of Contents

A. Understanding Money 1

A1: Life Cycle of a U.S. Dollar 3

A2: Features of the Dollar 5

A3: Banking with Bucks 7

A4: Loans, Lenders, and Borrowers 9

A5: Money is History 11

A6: Dollars and Sense 13

A7: Strange Change 15

A8: Being Smart about Money 17

A9: Money Talk 19

A10: Does FREE Mean $0 Cost? 21

A11: Money Time 23

A12: Expense Overload 25

A13: My Word or My Collateral 27

A14: What Would You Do? 29

B. Making Money 31

B1: Be Your Own Boss 33

B2: Totally Taxed 35

B3: Money and Happiness 37

B4: Getting Paid 39

B5: Anatomy of a Pay Stub 41

B6: Who is Uncle Sam? 43

B7: Pay Day! 45

C. Saving Money 47

C1: Size Matters 49

C2: My Mind and My Money 51

C3: Rent versus Own 53

C4: Saving Money 55

C5: Money Earned, Money Saved! 57

C6: Would You Rather? 59

C7: Making Your Money Last 61

C8: Making More of Your Money Last 63

C9: Bargain Shopping 65

C10: Bartering for Bargains 67

C11: Needs versus Wants 69

C12: Save or Spend? 71

C13: Price versus Cost 73

D. Spending Money **75**

    D1:   Check Yourself 77

    D2:   Debit Card versus. Credit Card 79

    D3:   Bad Money Habits 81

    D4:   Money Magic 83

    D5:   Feed Me! 85

    D6:   Planning for the Future 87

    D7:   Cash Money 89

    D8:   Discipline with Money 91

    D9:   The Deal Maker 93

    D10: Bills, Bills, Bills! 95

    D11: Budgeting (What, Why, When) 97

    D12: Budgeting 101 99

    D13: Credit Cards 101

    D14: It Costs How Much? 103

Answer Key **105**

About the Author 121

Also by Al Riddick 123

UNDERSTANDING MONEY

The Life Cycle of a U.S. Dollar

What you will learn today:
- Name of the government agency responsible for printing U.S. paper currency
- Role of Federal Reserve Banks in the life cycle of a U.S. dollar
- How U.S. currency ends up in your hands

Instructions:
This lesson will explain the different stages the dollar passes through from the time it is created until it is eventually destroyed. Each of the pictures in the circle represents a step in the life cycle of a dollar:

- **Consumers**
- **Federal Reserve Banks (FRB)**
- **Commercial Banks**
- **Bureau of Engraving and Printing (BEP)**

Draw a line from the picture to where it belongs on the life cycle. **Hint:** Two of the pictures will be used twice.

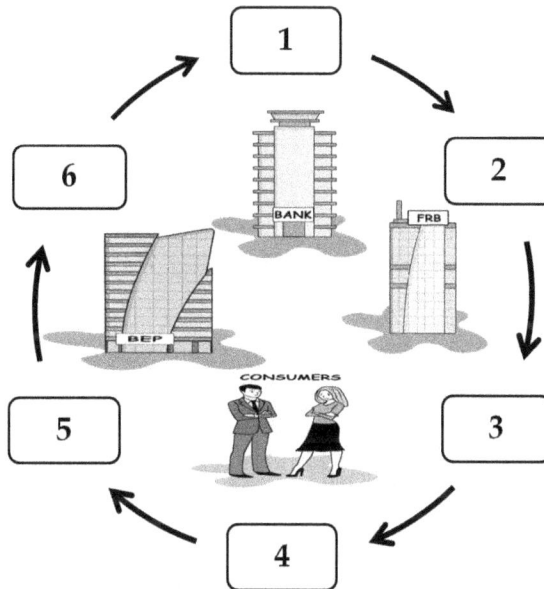

Did you know?
- US paper money is 75% cotton and 25% linen.
- Of the notes the Federal Reserve receives on deposit, about one-third are not fit for future circulation.
- The average life span of $1, $5, $10 and $20 bills is less than two years.

Features of the Dollar

What you will learn today:

- Items featured on the front of a U.S. dollar

Instructions:

Look at the picture of the U.S. dollar below. Match the question number to the correct box on the picture:

1. Where is the Federal Reserve seal?
2. Where is the serial number?
3. Who is the person featured on the front?
4. Where is the U.S. Treasury seal?
5. Where is the Secretary of the Treasury signature?
6. Where is the Treasurer of the United States signature?

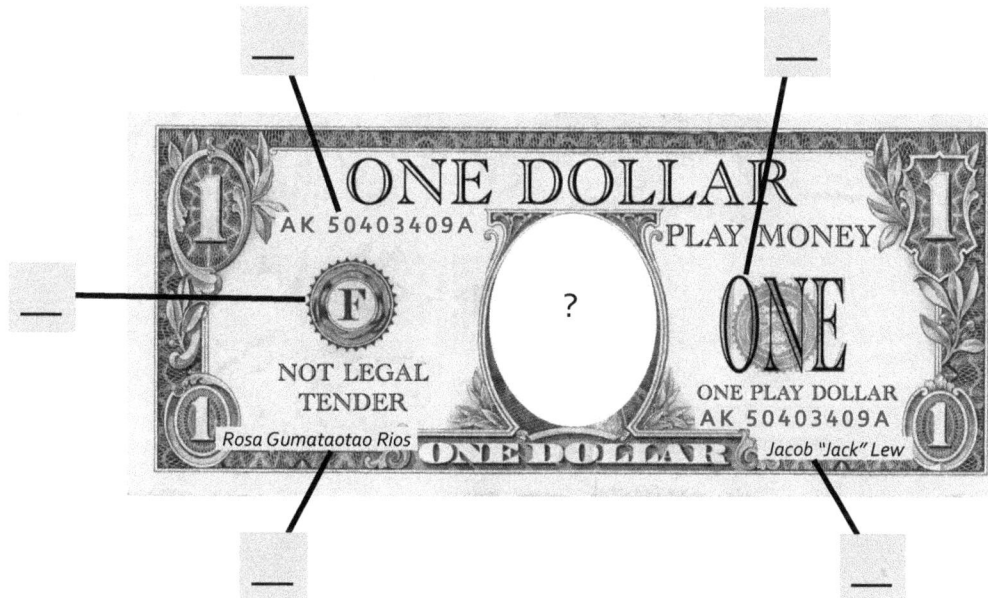

Banking with Bucks

What you will learn today:

The basic functions of a bank

1. **Storing money**—accepting deposits into customers' banking accounts
2. **Lending money**—allowing customers to borrow money (interest is charged on money borrowed)
3. **Executing a financial transaction**—assisting customers with electronic or paper transactions involving their banking accounts

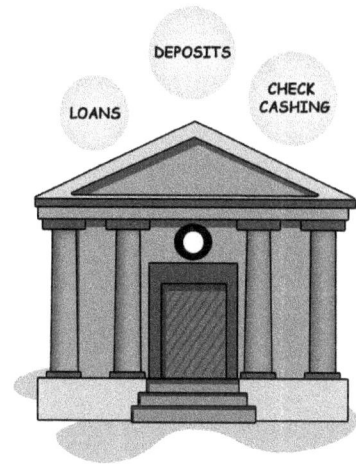

Instructions:

Determine which banking function from the list above best describes the following transactions. Place a check mark in the appropriate box.

Items	Storing money	Lending money	Executing a financial transaction
Making a deposit in a savings account			
Writing a check for groceries			
Applying for and receiving an auto loan			
Making a deposit in a checking account			
Applying for and receiving a mortgage (loan for a house)			
Cashing a check			
Paying for a pair of shoes with a debit card			
Paying for a pair of jeans with a bank credit card			

Loans, Lenders, and Borrowers

What you will learn today:

The pros and cons of borrowing money

Terms you need to know:

- **Loan**–the act of borrowing money
  Lender–an organization or person who lends money
  Borrower–an organization or person who receives a loan

Discussion Questions:

Why do you think people borrow money?

What do people borrow money to buy?

When people use credit cards, do you think they are borrowing money?

What do you think happens when you don't have the money to pay a bank or credit card company back for the money they loaned you?

What's the word used to describe the cost of borrowing?

Money is History

What you will learn today:
Name of person pictured on your money

Instructions:
Match the name of the person with the bill on which their face appears.

Featured Picture	What bill am I on?
Abraham Lincoln	
Alexander Hamilton	
Andrew Jackson	
Ulysses S. Grant	
Benjamin Franklin	

1. How many of these men are not past U.S. Presidents? Can you name them?

    _____

    _____

2. Which of these men was the first U.S. Secretary of the Treasury?

    _____

    _____

3. Can you name the 7th President of the U.S.?

    _____

    _____

4. Who was the sixteenth President of the U.S.?

    _____

    _____

5. Which of the men on U.S. paper currency is one of the Founding Fathers of the U.S.?

    _____

    _____

Did you know?

Thomas Jefferson, our third President, is featured on the $2 bill. This bill is not discussed here because of its infrequent use.

Dollars and Sense

. . . .

What you will learn today:

Math and money make a good couple

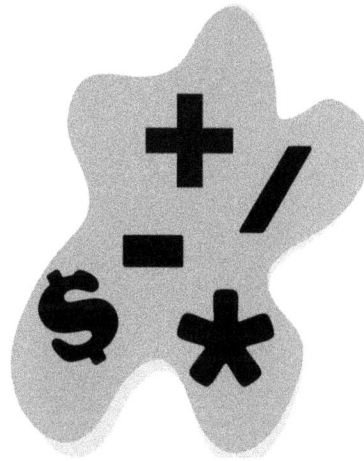

Figure it out:

Would you rather have a penny every hour for one week or one dollar for one week?

Would you rather have $10 everyday for one year or $5 every six hours for one year?

Strange Change

. . . .

What you will learn today:

How creative you are with numbers and math skills

Instructions:

Think of as many ways as possible to make a dollar using change. For example, four quarters ($.25 X 4) equals $1 and ten dimes ($.10 X 10) equals $1. The coins to be used for this exercise include: penny, nickel, dime, quarter and half dollar.

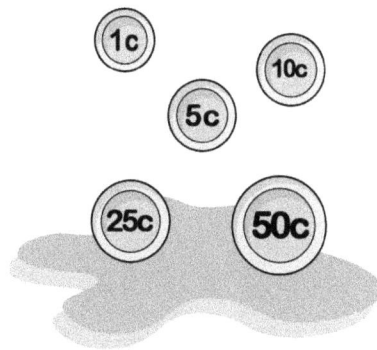

Hint: There are 293 different ways to make change for $1 using the coins listed above. Good luck!

Being Smart about Money

What you will learn today:

The potential impact of intelligence and work habits on your money

Discussion Questions:

1. What is the relationship between intelligence and work habits?

2. What would it mean if you heard someone say, "(insert your name) is a hard worker?"

3. Do you think it's better to be smart and lazy or to be a hard working person? Why?

4. What do you think the word *lazy* means?

Money Talk

What you will learn today:

Common terminology used when talking about money

Instructions:

This word search puzzle is based on everyday words people use when talking about money. Some words may be spelled diagonally or backwards. Enjoy the search.

```
S  K  Z  E  D  N  U  F  E  R  N  H  S  C
S  O  V  Z  V  V  C  A  S  P  Y  G  A  Z
I  I  P  R  Z  I  N  T  E  R  E  S  T  B
G  R  S  Q  P  F  J  O  P  U  X  I  U  V
Q  T  R  E  Q  R  F  T  V  Y  K  D  M  S
R  A  A  W  C  C  O  Y  T  R  G  X  N  F
J  X  L  L  E  I  C  Q  O  E  Y  K  W  F
L  E  L  O  T  A  O  W  T  P  I  C  S  Z
C  S  O  E  J  X  L  H  Y  F  A  E  A  D
H  S  D  M  Y  Y  L  T  C  I  D  H  V  N
F  T  K  O  J  L  I  J  H  F  J  C  E  E
S  N  T  C  R  E  C  E  I  P  T  Y  L  P
H  E  E  N  B  H  D  O  Q  J  O  A  F  S
G  C  S  I  J  O  D  J  Z  T  X  P  X  O
```

budget	income	save
cents	interest	spend
choice	receipt	taxes
dollars	refund	wealth
give	paycheck	work

If you don't know all the definitions of these words, congratulations, you now have homework.

Does FREE Mean $0 Cost?

What you will learn today:

The word FREE can sometimes be associated with a cost

Instructions:

Decide if you want to work for one week as a waiter at a restaurant or as a salesperson at a shoe store. Let's pretend your best friend comes to your job to visit. Luckily, your friend wins a FREE dinner for two or a FREE pair of gym shoes.

Question: Who pays for the FREE dinner and FREE shoes?

Additional questions:

1. If you bought something for someone and he broke it or threw it in the trash, how would that make you feel?

2. How should another person's property that was given to you for free be treated?

3. If you bought a product from the internet because it featured a FREE SHIPPING offer, who pays to ship your product?

Money Time

. . . .

What you will learn today:

How much knowledge you have of basic financial terminology

Instructions:

Complete the crossword puzzle below to determine your level of financial understanding.

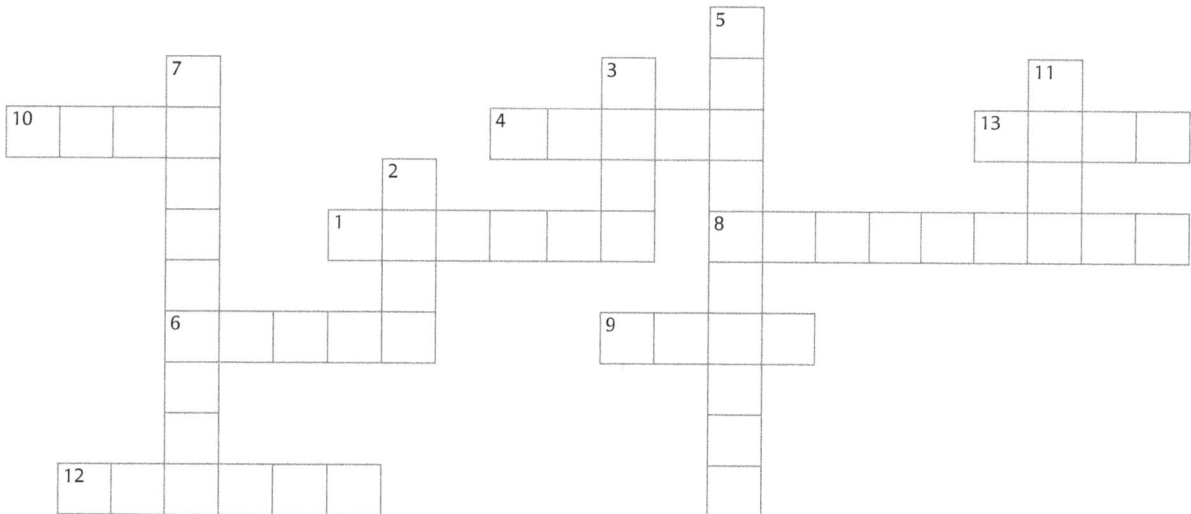

Across:

1. four quarters; ten dimes; twenty nickels

4. having completely run out of money

6. method of payment used when you don't have a debit card, credit card, or money order

8. forced contribution to the federal and state governments based on money earned

9. having a great deal of money; wealthy

10. when you don't spend money

12. written plan to determine income and expenses for a specific period of time

13. financial institution that collects deposits, makes loans, and helps consumers execute financial transactions

Down:

2. what mostly everyone in the U.S. must do to earn money

3. not earning a salary but paid by the _____

5. type of payment method that allows you to buy things when you don't have money but charges interest when you don't pay off your balance in full

7. type of payment method that is usually linked to a checking account

11. opposite of need

Expense Overload

. . . .

What you will learn today:

To understand the decision making process when expenses are more than income for a month

Instructions:

Pretend you are preparing your monthly budget and discover your expenses are more than the amount of money you bring home. In this exercise, you will determine what items to eliminate from next month's expenses so you will not overspend. Here's a sample of next month's budget.

Income:

Job:	$1,000

Expenses:

Entertainment:	$200
Cell Phone Bill:	$100
Grocery:	$300
Clothing:	$200
Rent:	$300
Car Payment:	$200

1. What will you eliminate or spend less money on to ensure your expenses don't exceed your income for the upcoming month?

2. What is the total amount spent on expenses after making adjustments so you don't overspend?

3. How did you determine what changes to make so your expenses would not be more than your income?

My Word or My Collateral

What you will learn today:

To understand the difference between secured credit/debt (when you pledge something as security for borrowing money) and unsecured credit/debt (when you don't have to pledge something as security when you borrow)

Questions:

What do you think happens when people don't pay their bills for months in a row?

_____

_____

How do you define the word *collateral?* Please provide an example.

_____

_____

Instructions:

Review the following examples and determine if the item is being bought with secured credit (collateralized), unsecured credit (uncollateralized), or neither.

Examples	Secured Credit	Unsecured Credit	Neither
Buying a new cell phone with a credit card			
Buying a new outfit with a gift card			
Buying a car by taking out a loan			
Taking out a student loan to pay for your college education			
Using a debit card to buy an iTunes gift card			
Taking out a loan to buy a house			
Buying a new pair of shoes with cash			

What Would You Do?

What you will learn today:

How understanding the principles of right and wrong can impact the decisions you make with money

Instructions:

Answer the following questions to understand that money is neither good nor bad. It's the decisions people make with money that count.

Pretend you are walking through the mall, and you see a $100 bill fall out of the pocket of the person in front of you.

1. Do you pick it up and put it in your pocket or return it to the person who dropped it? Why?

2. How would your answer be different if you were the person who dropped the $100 bill?

3. What if the person who dropped the $100 bill was homeless? How would that impact your answer?

4. Can you describe a decision you made with money that you would do differently if you had the chance? Explain your answer.

MAKING
MONEY

Be Your Own Boss

What you will learn today:
To utilize your creativity while developing an idea for a product

Instructions:
You have the opportunity to invent a new product. It can only make a profit (amount remaining after you subtract expenses from income) if the selling price is more than what it costs you to produce the product.

Determine the following:

1. What is the name of your product?

2. How does it work?

3. Who will you sell your product to?

4. How much does it cost to make (manufacture) your product?

5. What is the selling price of your product?

Totally Taxed

What you will learn today:

The definition of tax and that paying taxes are a part of everyday adult life

Instructions:

Place the correct alphabet of the following words beside the appropriate definition.

A. Sales tax
B. Income tax
C. Property tax
D. Payroll tax
E. Corporate tax

	Tax employers withhold and/or pay on behalf of their employees based on the wage or salary of the employee
	Tax based on the cost of the item purchased that is collected directly from the buyer
	Tax that must be paid by a corporation based on the amount of profit (revenue minus expenses) it generates
	Tax on the money a person earns from doing his job or operating his business
	Tax applied against the owner of real estate based on the value of the property

Money and Happiness

What you will learn today:

Making money is more fun when you enjoy what you do for a living

Instructions:

Answer the following questions to better understand how to match things you enjoy with a possible job opportunity.

What are some of the things you enjoy doing?

_____

_____

_____

Make a list of things you've been told you do well.

_____

_____

_____

Exercise questions:

1. Do you think it's better to make a lot of money doing a job you don't like or make a normal (whatever that means to you) amount of money doing something you enjoy? Explain your answer.

_____

_____

_____

2. What is something you enjoy doing so much that you would do it for free?

_____

_____

_____

3. Does it matter more to be a good person or make a lot of money? Explain your answer.

_____

_____

_____

4. Do people who make a lot of money deserve to be treated any differently than people who don't? Why?

_____

_____

_____

Getting Paid

What you will learn today:

The different ways you can be paid to do a job

Instructions:

In the examples below, determine how each of the workers gets paid. Your choices are: Hourly, Commission, Salary, Pieceworker, Overtime, Bonus. Some questions will have more than one answer.

Questions:

1. John works as a car salesman and earns $500 for every car he sells. Does he get paid by the hour, a salary, or work on commission?

2. Jane works as a medical assistant at a doctor's office and earns $20 for each hour she works. What type of worker is she?

3. Mary is the President of a bank and earns $75,000 a year. Mary works 50 hours some weeks and 70 hours during other weeks. What type of worker is Mary?

4. Mike works as a manager at a restaurant. He earns $50,000 a year no matter how many hours he works. He also gets a bonus if his restaurant sales more food in one month than it did as compared to the previous month. How is Mike paid?

5. Tracy earns $.10 for every computer chip she installs during an 8 hour shift. What type of worker is she?

6. Toni earns twice her hourly pay when she works more than 40 hours in a week. How is Toni paid?

Anatomy of a Pay Stub

What you will learn today:

Common features of a paystub and how they impact your take home pay

Instructions:

From the information provided, determine the gross pay and the amount of money remaining after deducting each of the categories below.

> Number of hours worked—160 (one month)
> Hourly pay—$25 per hour

INCOME	
Gross Pay for Total Hours Worked	$
DEDUCTIONS	
Federal Income Tax—25% of Gross Pay	$
Pre-tax retirement—10% of Gross Pay -	$
Automatic Deposit to Savings—5% of Gross Pay	$
Social Security—4% of Gross Pay	$
State Income Tax—3% of Gross Pay	$
Medicare—2% of Gross Pay	$
NET PAY (Amount you would take home)	$

Note: Percentages used are fictitious and may not reflect the actual amounts for federal and state taxes.

Who is Uncle Sam?

. . . .

What you will learn today:

More about the impact of taxes and the nickname given to the U.S. government

Instructions:

Pretend you have ten $100 bills ($1,000) representing your total pay for two weeks. Calculate the amount of taxes you owe based on the following rates which are applied to your gross pay.

Federal Income Tax	20%	
State Income Tax	5%	
Social Security Tax	4%	
Medicare Tax	2%	

Questions:

1. How much money do you have left after paying taxes?

_____

_____

_____

2. Do you think having to pay taxes is fair? Why or why not?

_____

_____

_____

3. What is federal income tax?

_____

_____

_____

4. What do you think happens if you don't pay your taxes?

_____

_____

_____

5. What do you think the word _Medicare_ means?

_____

_____

_____

6. What is your definition of the phrase _social security_?

_____

_____

_____

7. Where do you think the U.S. government should spend most of the money it collects? Why?

_____

_____

_____

Pay Day!

What you will learn today:

The different ways in which you can receive a paycheck including the pros and cons of each

Instructions:

The following questions will help you understand popular methods for receiving a paycheck

1. Pretend you have a full time job. What are the different ways in which you can receive payment from your job?

2. What do you think are the advantages and disadvantages of getting paid by paper check? By cash? By direct deposit?

Payment Method	Advantages	Disadvantages
Paper Check		
Cash		
Direct Deposit		

SAVING
MONEY

Size Matters

. . . .

What you will learn today:

How to determine what size of a particular product gives you the best value for your money

Instructions:

In each example below, determine which size product is the best deal. Circle your choice.

Potato Chips

One 1 ounce snack size bag =$1.00

One 2 ounce single serve bag =$1.80

One 10 ounce large bag = $2.50

Bottle of water

8 ounces=$.50

16 ounces=$3.00

32 ounces=$4.00

Cheeseburger

One 1 pound cheeseburger=$1.00

Two 8 ounce cheeseburgers=$1.00

Three 1 pound cheeseburgers=$2.00

Note: The grocery store shelf tag usually details the cost per unit price. This makes it easier to compare prices quickly while shopping. When a product is larger, it is usually believed to be a better value. However, if the cost per unit is higher for the larger product than for the smaller product, the better deal is the smaller item.

My Mind and My Money

What you will learn today:

Commonly used financial terms which have a positive financial outcome

Instructions:

Complete the crossword puzzle to understand words associated with having a positive money mentality.

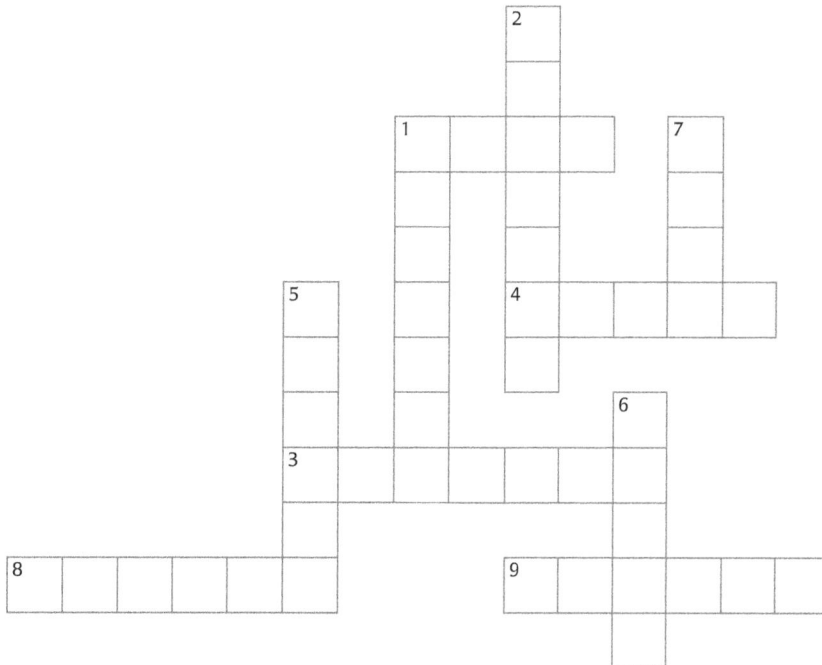

Across:

1. something you do to words in a book

3. the opposite of impatient

4. _____ before you speak

8. If you stop talking, then you can ____.

9. written plan to track income and expenses for a specific period

Down:

1. _____ your elders

2. _____ versus quantity

5. used to get a discount on a product or service

6. If you don't _____, you might fail your test.

7. detailed way of doing something; game____

Rent versus Own

What you will learn today:
How to use math to determine if it's best to rent or buy a product

Instructions:
Pretend you have a full time job and are living on your own. You have an apartment but are in need of a bed. Here are your two options:

(A) Rent a bed for $50 a month for a minimum of 18 months or

(B) Save money from each paycheck at a rate of $100/week for four weeks and pay cash.

Which option would you choose and why?

_____

_____

_____

Additional questions:

1. Where would you sleep if you didn't have a bed?

   _____

   _____

   _____

2. What's the difference in cost associated with sleeping on the floor for four weeks versus renting a bed?

   _____

   _____

   _____

3. What could you do with the money saved by not renting a bed?

   _____

   _____

   _____

Saving Money

What you will learn today:

It's not how much you earn, it's how much you save.

Instructions:

Please answer the following questions to understand your views about saving money.

1. What does saving money mean to you?

2. Why do you think some people save money and some people don't?

3. What are some of the advantages of saving money?

4. Describe how someone who has a job can save money.

5. What are some of the bad things that can happen when you don't save money?

Money Earned, Money Saved!

What you will learn today:

Just because you make a lot of money doesn't mean you have a lot of money.

Instructions:

Answer the following questions to understand why saving money is just as important as making money.

Questions:

1. When you get a job, do you think it's important to make a lot of money? Why?

2. What amount do you consider to be a lot of money to be paid for a job? Why?

3. What are your thoughts about making a lot of money and spending all the money you make?

4. If you had to choose, would you prefer to make a normal amount of money and have good money habits (saving, budgeting, planning for retirement) or make a lot of money but not use it correctly (not saving, not living on a budget, not planning for retirement)? Why?

Would You Rather?

. . . .

What you will learn today:

You can work hard for money but money can also work hard for you.

Instructions:

Provide definitions for the following words, and then answer the question to test your understanding.

Interest	
Compound interest	

Here's an example of compounding interest:

Timing	Amount	
Start	$1	
Year 1	$1 + 10% ($.10) = **$1.10**	
Year 2	$1.10 + 10% ($.11) = **$1.21**	
Year 3	$1.21 + 10% ($.12) = **$1.33**	

Question: Would you prefer to put $1 a day for 60 days in a cookie jar or $30 once in an account that earns 10% interest *each* month for the next 12 months? Be able to support your answer using math.

Making Your Money Last

What you will learn today:

There is usually an extra cost associated with buying name brand products.

Tip: A brand is the name, term, design, or symbol of a specific seller's product, service, or business. For example, when you think about gym shoes, what are some brands that come to mind?

Instructions:

Answer the following questions to better understand what you think about brand name and non-name brand products.

1. What do you think of when you hear the phrase *name brand*?

2. Can you name some products you consider to be name brand?

3. Do you think name brand products are better than non-name brand products? Why?

4. Why do you think name brand products usually cost more than non-name brand products?

5. When you buy your first car, do you plan to buy a name brand car or something that may be less costly but more affordable for your budget?

Note: Denim is used to make jeans. Denim may be inexpensive but once a certain name is attached to a pair of jeans, they might cost more.

Making More of Your Money Last

What you will learn today:

Saving a small percentage of your paycheck each month might add up to a lot of money over time.

Instructions:

Answer the following questions to gain an understanding of why it's important to save a small portion from each paycheck.

1. Since most adults work very hard for the money they earn, do you think they should save a small portion from each paycheck? Why?

2. If you earned $500 a week on your job, how much do you think you should save each month? Why?

3. If you saved a small amount of money from each paycheck for all the years you plan to work (e.g., 20 years, 30 years), how might that impact your life?

4. What do you think would be the advantage of having a savings goal for the amount of money you bring home in each paycheck?

5. What do you think it means to pay yourself first?

Bargain Shopping

What you will learn today:

To become familiar with bargain shopping and understand how it can save you money

Instructions:

Answer the following questions to become familiar with how you feel about bargain shopping.

1. What do you think the word *bargain* means?

2. Can you name some items you may want to buy and receive a bargain? Why?

3. Do you think it's possible to be so concerned about receiving a bargain that you waste money? Explain your answer.

4. What do you think people mean when they say, "time is money"? Provide an example.

5. Do you think it's best to pay full price for something or wait until the item you want goes on sale? Why?

Bartering for Bargains

What you will learn today:

Bartering can be a good way to save money.

Hint: You will need a partner to complete this exercise.

Instructions:

Please define the following term to assist in your understanding of the bartering process.

Bartering:

Now, it's time to apply your knowledge in a real-life barter transaction. First, make a list of some items or services you would like to receive in your transaction. Some examples are listed below:

1. Help in a subject at school
2. Tips to achieve high scores in a video game
3. Dance lessons

Next, make a list of some things you would be willing to exchange for the item/service you receive above. A few suggestions are included below:

1. PSP/Xbox/Wii game
2. Name brand clothing
3. Lessons in a particular sport

Review your lists and think of some people who have the items/skills you desire. Be sure you have something to offer that the other person would be interested in. ***Discuss your idea with a parent prior to approaching anyone***. Record details of your first barter transaction here:

Needs versus Wants

What you will learn today:

To understand the difference between a need and a want and be able to provide examples

Instructions:

Please provide definitions of the following terms:

Needs:	
Wants:	

List at least five examples of needs and fives examples of wants.

Needs examples	Wants examples

Questions:

What can happen to your money when wants are considered needs?

_____

_____

_____

What have you desired in the past that was a want but you thought it was a need?

_____

_____

_____

Save or Spend?

What you will learn today:

It's best to keep your emotions under control when making financial decisions.

Instructions:

It's your lucky day. The manager on your pretend job has just given you a $500 bonus for being named employee of the month. Please answer the following questions.

1. How do you decide what to do with the money? How did you determine your answer?

2. How would your answer change if you didn't have any money in your savings account? In other words, if you were broke?

3. How would your answer change if you had hit your savings goal for the year and didn't need to save more money?

4. What would you do if your best friend found out about your bonus and asked you to "give" him $100 because he lost money playing a game at the casino? Why?

Price versus Cost

What you will learn today:

Buying an item on credit can cost you more than the actual sticker price

Instructions:

Provide definitions for the following terms:

Price:	
Cost:	

You have the opportunity to purchase a new pair of $100 gym shoes. There are three different options to consider when paying. Determine the true cost of the gym shoes given the interest rates provided. Which option provides the best deal?

Option A: Price: $100 (pay off over 9 months at 15% interest) =	
Option B: Price: $100 (pay off over 6 months at 10% interest) =	
Option C: Price: $100 (pay off over three months at 5% interest) =	

MONEY $MART TEENS · · · 73

SPENDING
MONEY

Check Yourself

What you will learn today:

How to write a check

Instructions:

Today's lesson will allow you to spend all the money you can imagine. Think of something you want to buy (it can be anything). Determine how much the particular item you are purchasing costs and who/where you are buying it from. Use this information to complete the check.

John B. Free
1234 Debt Free Lane
Money Smart Teens, USA 12345

1234

Date: _____

$ [_____]

Pay to the order of

_____ Dollars

Financial Institution
Money-town, USA 12345

Memo _____   _____

012123321   12345678   1234

Pay to the order of: This is where you write the name of the person or company to whom you will write the check. Always draw a line to the end which prevents someone else from writing an additional name on your check.

Dollars: This is where you write the amount of the check in words. For example, a $200 check would be written as—two hundred and 00/100.

012123321—Represents the 9 digit bank code (i.e., routing number) that associates a specific financial institution with an account. **12345678**—Represents the account number at the financial institution. **1234**—Check number.

Memo: Reminder of why you wrote the check (optional)

Signature Line: Where you sign your name

Debit Card versus Credit Card

What you will learn today:

The difference between a debit card and a credit card

Instructions:

Provide definitions of *debit card* and *credit card* in the boxes below.

Debit Card	Credit Card

Determine if a debit card or credit card is the best method to pay for items on the list below. Place a check mark in the appropriate box.

Items	Debit Card	Credit Card
Grocery		
Gas for your car		
Cell phone bill		
Electricity bill		
New outfit		
Plane ticket		
Gym shoes		
Movie tickets		
Concert tickets		
Video games		

Bad Money Habits

What you will learn today:
Common terminology used when talking about money in a negative way

Instructions:
This word search puzzle is based on everyday words people use when talking about money in a negative way. Some words may be spelled diagonally or backwards. Happy searching!

```
U A S W I B B E Q A Q M T N T C H
E W D Z S T M V S X X E N I F H S
K N N Y R H Q N M S X X S B S E A
K K U G S A F D E B T D H T R C C
I K F U E T U R A O E K O R B K S
T U T U N N W O O T T N E R D T A
V Z N B S N A O L Y A D Y A P O E
U D E I J O O P V O E F F D U C M
O W I M M U L Z H X I O U Q G H A
S W C V O N C F H R C C C S R E S
G N I P P O H S E S L U P M I C B
U G F L R Y T L A N E P M W T K I
D Y F C M N O M O N E Y D O W N X
Q Q U G T N E M Y A P E T A L H G
I S S W G R E C N A V D A H S A C
I P N D J F J D W D N N E T J N C
Z M I T F A R D R E V O A K Z O Z
```

broke	impulse shopping	payday loan
cash advance	insufficient funds	penalty
check to check	late payment	rent to own
debt	no money down	same as cash
fine	overdraft	

If you don't know all the definitions of these words, congratulations, you now have more homework.

Money Magic

. . . .

What you will learn today:
How money can appear and disappear…just like magic

Instructions:
It often takes a lot of work to make money appear, but it takes very little effort to make it disappear. For example, it could take someone two weeks to make $1,000. If he decided to visit a casino and gamble, all his money could be gone very quickly. Place the alphabet associated with the following words beside the appropriate definition.

a. Sales Commission
b. Net Pay
c. Gross Pay
d. Hourly Pay
e. Salary
f. Budget
g. Savings
h. Emergency Fund

_____ money earned by sales people based on the amount of products, goods, or services they convince others to purchase

_____ money set aside to pay for something you don't know will happen in the future (e.g., going to the dentist because you chipped a tooth eating too much candy, breaking your eye glasses, accidentally dropping and breaking your laptop)

_____ type of pay earned based on hours worked

_____ money set aside to pay for something you want to buy in the future (e.g., video games, new cell phone, or clothes)

_____ the amount of money in your paycheck left over after deductions (i.e., taxes and other expenses)

_____ a written plan created to track income and expenses for a set period of time

_____ a set amount of pay earned regardless of the number of hours worked

_____ the amount of money in your paycheck before any deductions are taken out

Feed Me!

What you will learn today:

There are always consequences to every financial decision...some good and others not so good.

Instructions:

You forgot to do your budget for this month. As a result, you have only $15 for the next 5 days. This is your entire food budget and you currently have no groceries. From the list of items below, determine what you can purchase to eat for the next 5 days to ensure you don't go over your $15 budget.

Available items to purchase include:

Loaf of Bread: $2
Jar of Peanut Butter: $1
Jar of Jelly: $1
Bag of Rice: $1
Bag of Beans: $1
Carton of Eggs (12 eggs): $2
One whole chicken: $5

Your Shopping Cart:

Planning for the Future

What you will learn today:

Living on your own comes with more expenses than you might think.

Instructions:

Answer the following questions to help you understand what life is like for most adults regarding money, expenses, and planning for the future.

Questions:

1. What do you think are some of the things you will have to pay for once you become an adult?

2. Now that you know some of the things you will have to pay for in your adult life, how does that impact how you view money?

3. Now that you realize someone else is paying for mostly everything you use in life, how does that make you view this person?

4. How do you see yourself in the future when it comes to making, spending, and saving money? Why?

Cash Money

What you will learn today:
Advantages of paying for goods and services in cash

Instructions:
Answer the following questions to learn how you feel about paying for items in cash.

1. Why do you think some people don't use cash when they buy things?

2. Do you think there are any advantages to paying for something in cash? What?

3. What do you think it means to *negotiate*?

4. What products do you think people should never pay full price to buy? Why?

Discipline with Money

What you will learn today:

The role discipline can play when handling money

Instructions:

No matter what you do in life, discipline can be your secret weapon. For example, having discipline with your study habits can help you earn a high score on a test. Discipline also has a role in your money habits as well. Answer the following questions to determine how discipline and money can make a great team.

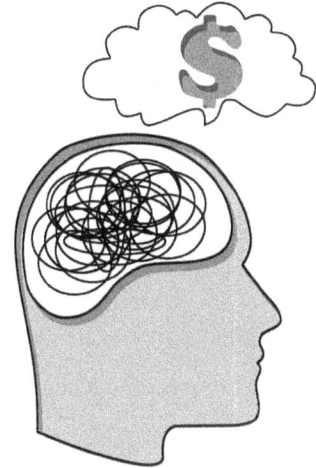

1. What does the word *discipline* mean to you?

2. Do you think you are a disciplined person? Why or why not?

3. Name something you do that requires discipline.

4. What role do you think discipline plays when making financial decisions?

5. If you give a person who is not disciplined $1,000 and give another person who is disciplined $1,000, what do you think would happen? Why?

The Deal Maker

. . . .

What you will learn today:

To evaluate an offer and determine what deal is best

Tip: Always think before you act when making financial decisions.

Instructions:

This exercise will help you practice how to identify a good deal. Read the following three options to determine which one is best and why.

1. Buy One, Get One FREE—Retail Price: $100 (second pair free)

2. Buy One, Get One 50% Off—Retail Price: $75 (second pair 50% off)

3. Buy two pair of gym shoes: 75% off the first pair and 50% off the second pair—Retail price: $100

Bills, Bills, Bills!

What you will learn today:

Become exposed to the concept of debt-free living

Instructions:

Answer the following questions to understand your feelings and attitudes regarding debt.

1. When you become an adult, do you think your life will be better off if you have a lot of debt or as little as possible? Why?

2. Think about how you would respond if you were told you could never borrow money. How would that impact the financial decisions you made on a day-to-day basis?

3. Do you think it's more difficult to live in debt or debt-free? Why?

4. How many advantages can you think of for people who choose to live debt-free?

5. What do you think are the disadvantages of living debt-free?

Budgeting (What, Why, When)

What you will learn today:

Your views about budgeting and why it can be beneficial

Instructions:

The following questions will help you understand how you relate to money and the budgeting process.

1. What does the word *budget* mean to you?

2. What have you heard about budgeting?

3. Do you think people who have a lot of money are good with budgeting? Why?

4. Do you think people who don't make a lot of money are good at the budgeting process? Why or why not?

5. When you start making money, do you plan on saving as much as possible or having as much fun as possible? Explain your answer. Based on your answer, describe what you think your life would be like in the next 20 years.

Budgeting 101

. . . .

What you will learn today:

How to create a budget

Instructions:

Please note the incomplete one month budget below. Your task is to spend all the *net pay* money so your budget will be complete. When you see a blank space, it's up to you to determine how much to spend. Remember: You have to spend all the money in your net pay so your balance (net pay−expenses) is $0. By doing this, you have given every dollar of your net pay an assignment. Don't forget to deduct expenses already listed.

Remember: If you don't train your money, it will misbehave.

Gross Pay: $4,000

Income (+)		
	Net Pay	$2,500
Expenses (−)		
	Charity	$
	Saving:	$
	Transportation: Car payment Gas Car Insurance	$400 $250 $100
	Housing:	$750
	Debt: Best Buy	$50
	Utilities: Cell Phone: Electricity: Water: Internet: Cable:	$100 $150 $50 $35 $40
	Food: Grocery	$
	Personal: (Hair, Clothes)	$
	Entertainment:	$

Credit Cards

. . . .

What you will learn today:
What a credit card is as well as the pros and cons of paying for something with a credit card

Instructions:
Answer the following questions to get a better understanding of how you view credit cards.

1. Do you think using a credit card is a good substitute for using your "real" money? Why?

2. Are you excited about being able to apply for a credit card when you get older? Why?

3. What do you think are the advantages of using a credit card?

4. What are the disadvantages of using a credit card?

5. Do you know anyone who does not use a credit card? If not, how do you think their life might be different from someone who does?

Tip: To get a better understanding, ask a few adults these questions and see how their answers compare to yours.

It Costs How Much?

What you will learn today:

The various ways a bill can be paid and the cost associated with each method

Instructions:

There are a number of ways a bill (i.e., cell phone, car payment, electricity) can be paid. Some ways are FREE and others may cost money. Complete the exercise below to determine what may be the least expensive *and* best way to pay bills.

Below are the costs associated with each method of paying a bill.

Money Order	$1.10
Stamp	$0.45
Write a check	$0.20
Cash payment	$20
Automatic Bank Draft (service provider is given access to your bank account and can withdraw funds even if the bill is incorrect)	$0
Pay Online (customer determines how much and when to pay service provider. Access to bank account is on a limited basis)	$0

Use the information provided above to compare expenses associated with paying a **$20 cable bill** in different ways.

	Total Cost (Bill + Payment Method)
Option 1: Mail Money Order =	
Option 2: Mail Check =	
Option 3: Automatic Bank Draft =	
Option 4: Pay On-line =	
Option 5: Mail Cash =	

What is the best and least expensive method?

ANSWER KEY

*(Discussion questions
purposely excluded)*

Assignment A1

Life Cycle of a U.S. Dollar

- **Step 1—Bureau of Engraving and Printing**—prints paper money and distributes it to Federal Reserve Banks
- **Step 2—Federal Reserve Banks**—distributes paper money to commercial banks (e.g., Bank of America, PNC Bank, Fifth Third Bank, Wells Fargo, JP Morgan Chase Bank) based on the amount the commercial bank requests
- **Step 3—Commercial Banks**—puts money in hands of consumers (typically by cashing checks or through automated teller machines)
- **Step 4—Consumers**—use money obtained from commercial banks to purchase goods and services
- **Step 5—Commercial Banks**—makes deposits to their federal reserve bank when they have excess paper money on hand
- **Step 6—Federal Reserve Bank**—destroys any paper money not fit for future use

Assignment A2

Features of the Dollar

Feature	Where it's located
1. Federal Reserve seal	Identified by alphabet F on left side
2. Serial number	AK50403409A
3. Person featured in portrait	George Washington (1st U.S. President)
4. U.S. Treasury seal	Right side, behind "ONE" and above serial no.
5. Secretary of the Treasury signature	Jacob "Jack" Lew (as of 2016)
6. Treasurer of the United States signature	Rosa Gumataotao Rios (as of 2016)

Assignment A3

Banking with Bucks

Items	Storing money	Lending money	Executing a financial transaction
Making a deposit in a savings account	X		
Writing a check for groceries			X
Applying for and receiving an auto loan		X	
Making a deposit in a checking account	X		
Applying for and receiving a mortgage (loan for a house)		X	
Cashing a check			X
Paying for a pair of shoes with a debit card			X
Paying for a pair of jeans with a bank credit card		X	

Assignment A5

Money is History

Currency	Featured Picture	Significance
$5	Abraham Lincoln	16th U.S. President
$10	Alexander Hamilton	1st U.S. Secretary of the Treasury (not a U.S. President)
$20	Andrew Jackson	7th U.S. President
$50	Ulysses S. Grant	18th U.S. President
$100	Benjamin Franklin	One of the Founding Fathers of the U.S.

1. How many of these men are not past U.S. Presidents?
   Answer: 2
   Can you name them?
   Answer: Alexander Hamilton and Benjamin Franklin
2. Which of these men was the first U.S. Secretary of the Treasury?
   Answer: Alexander Hamilton
3. Can you name the 7th President of the U.S.? **Answer:** Andrew Jackson
4. Who was the sixteenth President of the U.S.?
   Answer: Abraham Lincoln
5. Which of the men on U.S. paper currency is one of the Founding Fathers of the U.S.?
   Answer: Benjamin Franklin

Assignment A6

Dollars and Sense

Option 1: A penny every hour for one week
1 penny each hour for 24 hours = 24 pennies per day
24 pennies per day multiplied by 7 days (i.e. 1 week) = **168 pennies**

Option 2: One dollar for one week
1 dollar = **100 pennies**
Therefore, 168 pennies or **$1.68** is more than 100 pennies or **$1.00**.

The better choice would be one penny every hour for one week.

Question 2:

Would you rather have $10 everyday for one year or $5 every six hours for one year?

Option 1: $10 everyday for one year
$10/day x 365 days/year = **$3,650** in a year

Option 2: $5 every six hours for one year
24 hours/6 hours = 4 six hour periods in a 24 hour day
$5 x 4 six hour periods in a 24 hour day = $20 a day
$20 a day x 365 days/year = **$7,300** in a year

The better choice would be $5 every six hours for one year.

Assignment A7

Strange Change

Answer: There are 293 different ways to make change for $1. Ask each student how many ways he was able to create. Allow the student who has the most combinations to share his examples with the class. Instruct the other students to listen carefully so they can add additional ways to make change for a dollar to their list.

Assignment A9

. . . .

Money Talk

```
S K Z E D N U F E R N H S C
S O V Z V V C A S P Y G A Z
I I P R Z I N T E R E S T B
G R S Q P F J O P U X I U V
Q T R E Q R F T V Y K D M S
R A A W C C O Y T R G X N F
J X L L E I C Q O E Y K W F
L E L O T A O W T P I C S Z
C S O E J X L H Y F A E A D
H S D M Y Y L T C I D H V N
F T K O J L I J H F J C E E
S N T C R E C E I P T Y L P
H E E N B H D O Q J O A F S
G C S I J O D J Z T X P X O
```

Assignment A10

. . . .

Does FREE Mean $0 Cost?

Answer: The owner of the restaurant and the owner of the shoe store paid for the FREE dinner and FREE gym shoes. Even when something is FREE, it still has a cost associated with it. It may not have cost the recipient of the FREE item any money, but someone had to buy it in order to give it away.

Assignment A11

Money Time

					5 c				
7 d		3 h		r			11 w		
10 s a v e		b r o k e			13 b a n k
b		2 w		u		d		n	
i		1 d o l l a r	8 i n c o m e t a x
t		r			8 i			
6 c h e c k		9 r i c h			
a				c				
r				a				
12 b u d g e t		r				
				d				

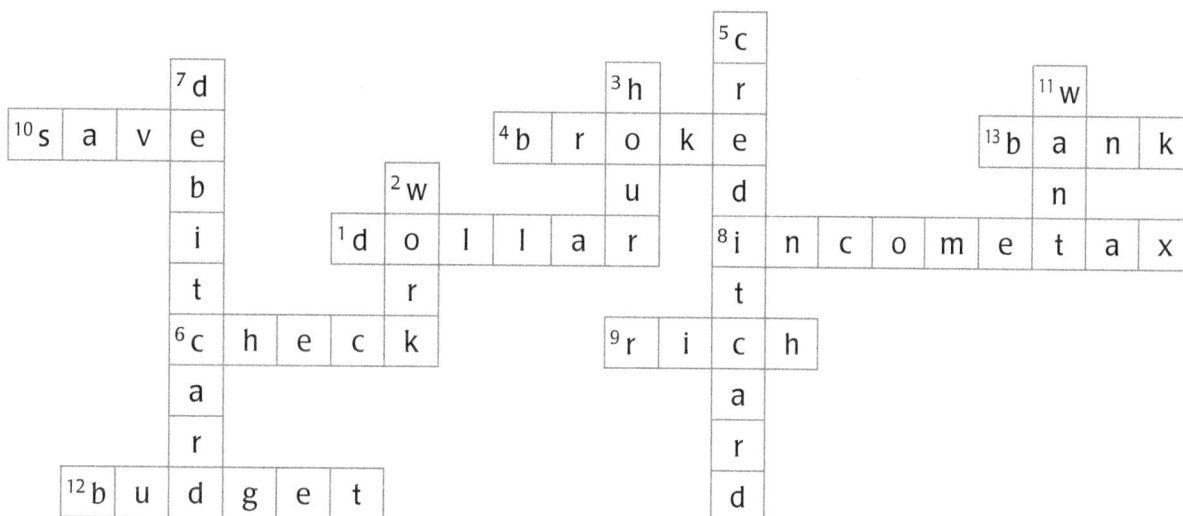

Assignment A12

Expense Overload

Answer: Expenses exceed income by $300. Students may decide to reduce/eliminate entertainment, grocery, or clothing for the month. Reducing the minutes on their cell phone plan could also save money.

Assignment A13

My Word or My Collateral

Collateral definition: something pledged as security for a loan

Collateral example: If you borrow money to buy a car, the car (i.e., collateral) is the pledge of security for the loan. If you don't pay your car payment, the bank has a right to take your car—even in the middle of the night.

Examples	Secured Credit	Unsecured Credit	Neither
Buying a new cell phone with a credit card		X	
Buying a new outfit with a gift card			X
Buying a car by taking out a loan	X		
Taking out a student loan to pay for your college education		X	
Using a debit card to buy an iTunes gift card			X
Taking out a loan to buy a house	X		
Buying a new pair of shoes with cash			X

Assignment B2

. . . .

Totally Taxed

- Payroll tax (D)—tax employers withhold and/or pay on behalf of their employees based on the wage or salary of the employee.
- Sales tax (A)—tax based on the cost of the item purchased that is collected directly from the buyer
- Corporate tax (E)—tax that must be paid by a corporation based on the amount of profit (revenue minus expenses) it generates
- Income tax (B)—tax on the money a person earns from doing his job or operating his business
- Property tax (C)—tax applied against the owner of real estate based on the value of the property

Assignment B4

. . . .

Getting Paid

1. John works as a car salesman and earns $500 for every car he sells. Does he get paid by the hour, a salary, or work on commission?
   Answer: Commission
2. Jane works as a medical assistant at a doctor's office and earns $20 for each hour she works. What type of worker is she?
   Answer: Hourly
3. Mary is the President of a bank and earns $75,000 a year. Mary works 50 hours some weeks and 70 hours during other weeks. What type of worker is Mary?
   Answer: Salary

4. Mike works as a manager at a restaurant. He earns $50,000 a year no matter how many hours he works. He also gets a bonus if his restaurant sales more food in one month than it did as compared to the previous month. How is Mike paid?
   Answer: Salary plus bonus (a payment added to what is usual)
5. Tracy earns $.10 for every computer chip she installs during an 8 hour shift.
   Answer: Pieceworker
6. Toni earns twice her hourly pay when she works more than 40 hours in a week.
   Answer: Hourly plus overtime

Assignment B5

Anatomy of a Pay Stub

Gross Pay for Total Hours Worked—**$4,000**
Federal Income Tax—25% of Gross Pay—**$1,000**
Pre-tax retirement—10% of Gross Pay—**$400**
Automatic Deposit to Savings—5% of Gross Pay—**$200**
Social Security—4% of Gross Pay—**$160**
State Income Tax—3% of Gross Pay—**$120**
Medicare—2% of Gross Pay—**$80**
Net Pay—**$2,040 (Amount student would take home)**

Assignment B6

Who is Uncle Sam?

Federal Income Tax—20% ($200)   State Income Tax—5% ($50)

Social Security Tax—4% ($40)   Medicare Tax—2% ($20)

Questions for students:

1. How much money do you have left after paying taxes? $1,000—($200 + $50 + $40 + $20) = **$690**
2. Do you think having to pay taxes is fair? Why or why not?
3. What is federal income tax?
   Answer: Tax imposed by the federal government based on the amount of income earned by individuals or businesses
4. What do you think happens if you don't pay your taxes?
   Possible answers: late payment penalties, fines (with interest), possible jail time, the government could stake a claim on your property (e.g., house, car, bank accounts)
5. What do you think the word *Medicare* means?
   Answer: A government program (i.e., social insurance program) in the U.S. created to provide guaranteed access to health insurance for seniors (people at least 65) and younger people with disabilities.

6. What is your definition of the phrase *social security*?
    Answer: Social security refers to the Old Age, Survivors, and Disability Insurance (OASDI) federal program. The largest component of OASDI is retirement benefits.

Assignment B7

. . . .

Pay Day!

1. Pretend you have a full time job. What are the different ways in which you can receive payment from your job?
    Possible answers: paper check, cash, direct deposit
2. What do you think are the advantages and disadvantages of getting paid by paper check? By cash? By direct deposit?
    Possible answers:
    Paper Check: Advantage—Funds are usually available at the time the check is deposited
    Disadvantages—could misplace the check; have to use gas driving to a bank to deposit the check
    Cash: Advantages—get the money immediately; don't have to visit a bank if you don't want to
    Disadvantages—could be robbed and all your money would be gone; having too much money in your pocket may get you excited about spending it
    Direct Deposit (i.e., when your employer can automatically put money in your bank account): Advantages—money is put directly in your bank account and usually available the morning of your pay date; it's safer
    Disadvantage—if your employer's or bank's electronic system is not working correctly, the money may not be deposited to your account on the day you expect

Assignment C1

. . . .

Size Matters

Potato Chips
One 1 ounce snack size bag = $1
One 2 ounce single serve bag = $1.80 ($.90/ounce)
One 10 ounce large bag = $2.50 ($.25/ounce) **best deal**

Bottle of water
$.50 for 8 ounces—**best deal**
$3 for 16 ounces = $1.50 per 8 ounces
$4 for 32 ounces = $1 per 8 ounces

Cheeseburger
One 1 pound cheeseburger—$1 ($1 per pound)
Two 8 ounce cheeseburgers—$1 ($1 for 1 pound; 16 ounces = 1 pound)
Three 1 pound cheeseburgers—$2 ($2/3 pounds = $.66/pound)—**best deal**

Assignment C2

My Mind and My Money

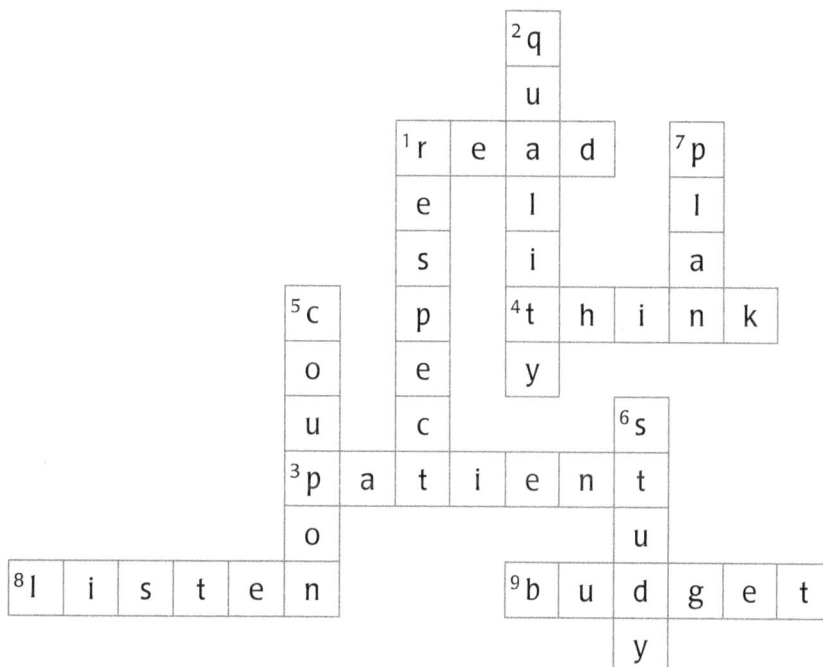

					[2]q								
					u								
			[1]r	e	a	d		[7]p					
			e		l			l					
			s		i			a					
		[5]c	p		[4]t	h	i	n	k				
		o	e		y								
		u	c					[6]s					
		[3]p	a	t	i	e	n	t					
		o						u					
[8]l	i	s	t	e	n			[9]b	u	d	g	e	t
								y					

Assignment C3

Rent versus Own

The correct answer is B. The better choice, based on financial reasoning, would be to save $400 over four weeks and buy a bed in cash. If option A was chosen, students would spend $900 ($50 X 18 months).

Assignment C6

Would You Rather?

Interest: a charge for the privilege of borrowing money; profit that is made on invested money

Compound Interest: earning interest from interest and principal (i.e., the total amount of money being lent or borrowed)

Answer: The best choice would be to put $30 once in an account that earns 10% interest each month for the next 12 months.

$30.00 + 10\% (\$3.00) = \$33.00$
$33.00 + 10\% (\$3.30) = \$36.30$
$36.30 + 10\% (\$3.63) = \$39.93$
$39.93 + 10\% (\$3.99) = \$43.92$
$43.92 + 10\% (\$4.39) = \$48.31$
$53.15 + 10\% (\$4.83) = \$53.14$
$53.14 + 10\% (\$5.31) = \$58.46$
$58.46 + 10\% (\$5.84) = \$64.30$
$64.30 + 10\% (\$6.43) = \$70.73$
$70.73 + 10\% (\$7.07) = \$77.81$
$77.81 + 10\% (\$7.78) = \$85.59$
$85.59 + 10\% (\$8.56) = \$94.15$

If you put $1 a day in a cookie jar for 60 days ($0 interest), you will only have $60.

Assignment C11

. . . .

Needs versus Wants

Answers: Needs are things people must have in order to stay alive. Wants are things people don't need to stay alive.

Needs Examples

food, shelter, clothing, oxygen

Wants Examples

iphone, video games, name brand gym shoes, name brand shirts and jeans, sports car, six bedroom house, iTunes gift card, laptop computer

Assignment C13

. . . .

Price versus Cost

Price—the amount of money you pay to buy something

Cost—the "total" amount of money associated with a purchase (e.g., price plus sales tax)

Answer: Option C is the best deal

Assignment D1

. . . .

Check Yourself (Seek assistance to determine if your check is written correctly.)

Assignment D2

Debit Card versus Credit Card

Debit Card—(also known as a **bank card** or **check card**) is a plastic card that provides the cardholder electronic access to his or her bank account(s) to withdraw cash or pay for goods and services. Credit Card—A plastic card issued by a bank, business, etc., for the purchase of goods or services on credit.

Answer: Given the choices provided, a **debit card** is the best way to pay for each of these items because the money must be in the student's bank account. The student could use a credit card, but if he doesn't have the money to pay the bill in full, he'll most likely have to pay a penalty called interest (i.e., price you pay for borrowed money).

Assignment D3

Bad Money Habits

```
U A S W I B B E Q A Q M T N T C H
E W D Z S T M V S X X E N I F H S
K N N Y R H Q N M S X X S B S E A
K K U G S A F D E B T D H T R C C
I K F U E T U R A O E K O R B K S
T U T U N N W O O T T N E R D T A
V Z N B S N A O L Y A D Y A P O E
U D E I J O O P V O E F F D U C M
O W I M M U L Z H X I O U Q G H A
S W C V O N C F H R C C C S R E S
G N I P P O H S E S L U P M I C B
U G F L R Y T L A N E P M W T K I
D Y F C M N O M O N E Y D O W N X
Q Q U G T N E M Y A P E T A L H G
I S S W G R E C N A V D A H S A C
I P N D J F J D W D N N E T J N C
Z M I T F A R D R E V O A K Z O Z
```

Assignment D4

. . . .

Money Magic

- **Sales Commission (A)**—money earned by sales people based on the amount of products, goods, or services they convince others to purchase
- **Emergency Fund (H)**—money set aside to pay for something you don't know will happen in the future (e.g., going to the dentist because you chipped a tooth eating too much candy, breaking your eye glasses, accidentally dropping and breaking your laptop)
- **Hourly Pay (D)**—type of pay earned based on hours worked
- **Savings (G)**—money set aside to pay for something you want to buy in the future (e.g., video games, new cell phone, clothes)
- **Net Pay (B)**—the amount of money in your paycheck left over after deductions (i.e., taxes and other expenses)
- **Budget (F)**—a written plan created to track income and expenses for a set period of time
- **Salary (E)**—a set amount of pay earned regardless of the number of hours worked
- **Gross Pay (C)**—the amount of money in your paycheck before any deductions are taken out

Assignment D5

. . . .

Feed Me!

Answer: As long as students spend $15 or less, any combination of answers will do.

Assignment D9

. . . .

The Deal Maker

1. Buy One, Get One FREE—Retail Price: $100 (second pair free); Total Cost = **$100**
2. Buy One, Get One 50% Off—Retail Price: $75 (second pair 50% off); Total Cost: $75 for first pair + $37.50 for second pair = **$112.50**
3. Buy two pair of gym shoes: 75% off the first pair and 50% off the second pair—Retail price: $100; Total Cost: $25 for first pair + $50 for second pair = **$75**
   Answer: Option 3 is the best deal

Assignment D13

. . . .

Credit Cards

Answer: Credit cards are pieces of plastic that allow people to borrow money to pay for things they want and/or think they need. Banks provide credit cards for people and typically charge them interest when they don't pay off their total bill each month.

Assignment D14

It Costs How Much?

Option 1: Mail Money Order: $1.10 (money order) + $.45 (stamp) + $20 (bill) = **$21.55**

Option 2: Mail Check: $.20 (check) + $.45 (stamp) + $20 (bill) = **$20.65**

Option 3: Automatic Bank Draft: $0 (no service fee) + $20 (bill) = **$20.00** (one of the least expensive, but not the *best* way)

Option 4: Pay On-line: $0 (no service fee) + $20 (bill) = **$20.00 (least expensive and best way)**

Option 5: Mail Cash: $.45 (stamp) + $20 (bill) = **$20.45**

(This option will probably end up costing **$40.45** because someone may steal the cash!)

About the Author

Al **Riddick** is President of **Game Time Budgeting** (GTB), a Cincinnati-based financial education firm. By the age of 33, Al and his wife (Lesia) achieved their *'debt-freedom'* goal. They have no mortgage, no school loans, no auto loans, and no credit card debt. Established in 2010, GTB helps individuals develop the proper mindset for spending less so they can have more. As a coach, speaker, guest columnist, and author, Al shares his passion for ***debt-free living*** by addressing the physical and emotional aspects of how people relate to money. Some of GTB's clients include Procter & Gamble, Toyota, Macy's, UPS, and Kroger. Game Time Budgeting was honored in 2015 as a *Cincinnati Children's Museum Difference Maker*.

Also by Al Riddick

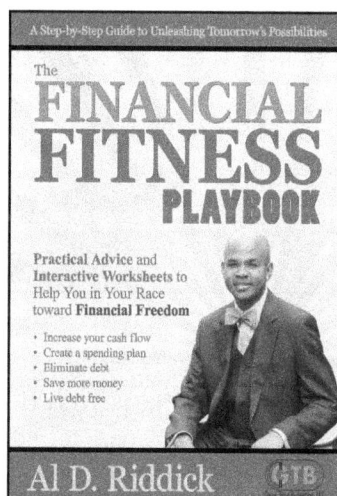

The Financial Fitness Playbook
A step-by-step guide to unleashing tomorrow's possibilities
(for adults and college students)

This workbook provides practical advice and interactive worksheets to assist on your journey to financial fitness. Each of the 14 lessons and training exercises will equip you with the proper money mindset, information, and tools to create a more favorable financial future.

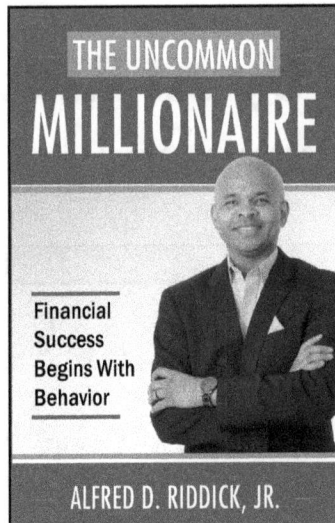

The Uncommon Millionaire
Financial Success Begins with Behavior

The *Uncommon Millionaire* reveals a small-town boy's journey from the North Carolina tobacco fields to achieving millionaire status in his late 30's. Al's common sense approach is mixed with humor accompanied by personal stories of financial challenge and triumph. His story captures your attention and prompts you to maximize your financial potential. Reading this book will help you understand how simple it is to take control of your financial life and create the outcomes you desire.

Get quantity discounts on orders of 25 or more copies.

www.GameTimeBudgeting.com

www.ingramcontent.com/pod-product-compliance
Lightning Source LLC
Chambersburg PA
CBHW062046090426
42740CB00016B/3042